Living with Weather

Robin Birch

Marshall Cavendish
Benchmark

New York

This edition first published in 2010 in the United States of America
by Marshall Cavendish Benchmark.

Marshall Cavendish Benchmark
99 White Plains Road
Tarrytown, NY 10591
www.marshallcavendish.us

First published in 2009 by
MACMILLAN EDUCATION AUSTRALIA PTY LTD
15–19 Claremont Street, South Yarra 3141

Visit our website at www.macmillan.com.au or go directly to www.macmillanlibrary.com.au

Associated companies and representatives throughout the world.

Library of Congress Cataloging-in-Publication Data

Birch, Robin.
    Living with weather / by Robin Birch.
        p. cm. – (Weather and climate)
    Summary: "Discusses how humans cope with the weather and climate of the area in which they live"–Provided by publisher.
    Includes bibliographical references and index.
    ISBN 978-0-7614-4465-7
    1. Weather–Effect of human beings on–Juvenile literature. I. Title.
    GF48.B58 2009
304.2'5–dc22

                                                                                2009004964

Edited by Kylie Cockle
Text and cover design by Marta White
Page layout by Marta White
Photo research by Legend Images
Illustrations by Gaston Vanzet

Printed in the United States

Acknowledgments
The author and the publisher are grateful to the following for permission to reproduce copyright material:
Front cover photograph: Building a snowman © George Muresan/Shutterstock
Photos courtesy of:
AAP/AP Photo/Lori Mehmen, 16 (bottom); © Mike Gillam/AUSCAPE, 22 (left); © Joe McDonald/AUSCAPE, 22 (right); ©
Anthonyata/Dreamstime.com, 26; © F2/Dreamstime.com, 23 (bottom); © Georgeburba/Dreamstime.com, 24 (right); © Grahamp/
Dreamstime.com, 5; © Jgroup/Dreamstime.com, 13 (top); © June-plum/Dreamstime.com, 24 (left); Juergen Schwarz/AFP/Getty
Images, 12 (bottom); Robert Caputo/Getty Images, 4; Frans Lemmens/Getty Images, 30; Ezra Shaw/Getty Images, 11; © Alain
Hennequin/iStockphoto, 13 (bottom); © Rob Newman/iStockphoto, 19 (top); © Mike Norton/iStockphoto, 25; © Peeter Viisimaa/
iStockphoto, 29; NASA/GFSC, 19 (bottom); Photolibrary/Steven Kazlowski, 23 (top); Photolibrary/OSF, 16 (top); Photolibrary/
Michael Sewell, 21 (bottom); Photolibrary/Joseph Sohm, 21 (top); Photolibrary/Tom Stewart, 12 (top); Photolibrary/The Print
Collector, 28; © afotoshop/Shutterstock, 10; © vera bogaerts/Shutterstock, 20 (right); © Alex James Bramwell/Shutterstock, 15;
© jam4travel/Shutterstock, 17; © Marcel Jancovic/Shutterstock, 6; © Seleznev Oleg/Shutterstock, 20 (left); © Regien Paassen/
Shutterstock, 7; © Steve Rosset/Shutterstock, 8; © sirano100/Shutterstock, 9 (right); © Marinko Tarlac/Shutterstock, 14; © Lee
Torrens/Shutterstock, 27; © Zdorov Kirill Vladimirovich/Shutterstock, 9 (left); © Lisa F. Young/Shutterstock, 18.

While every care has been taken to trace and acknowledge copyright, the publisher tenders their apologies for any accidental
infringement where copyright has proved untraceable. Where the attempt has been unsuccessful, the publisher welcomes
information that would redress the situation.

1 3 5 6 4 2

Contents

Glossary Words

When a word is printed in **bold**, you can look up its meaning in the Glossary on page 31.

Weather and Climate

What is the weather like today? Is it hot, cold, wet, dry, windy, or calm? Is it icy or snowy? Is there a storm on the way? We are all interested in the weather because it makes a difference in how we feel, what we wear, and what we can do.

The weather takes place in the air, and we notice it because air is all around us.

Climate

The word *climate* describes the usual weather of a particular place. If a place usually has cold weather, then we say that place has a cold climate. If a place usually has hot weather, we say it has a hot climate.

Weather Report

Most of Earth's weather happens between the ground and 7.5 miles (12 kilometers) up.

The Himba people of Namibia, Africa, live in a very hot and dry climate.

Living with Weather

People live in places on Earth that are hot, cold, wet, and dry.

In most cases, we wear clothes to protect us from the weather and keep us comfortable. Our houses and other buildings are built to suit the weather in our area.

A weather **forecast** helps us to be prepared for the weather. If we know what to expect, we can prepare for and be kept safe from dangerous weather.

Many communities have systems in place to help those in trouble during dangerous weather. These systems include rescue organizations, storm shelters, and storm warnings on the television and radio.

Weather forecasts are made by **meteorologists** and everyday people, who observe the weather and read weather maps.

Emergency crews are needed to help people clean up the wreckage caused by storms.

Clothes

People try to wear clothes that are suited to the weather so that they are comfortable and safe.

Cold-Weather Clothes

In cold weather we can keep warm by wearing our clothes in layers. The layers keep in the warmth. It is best to have three main layers.

- The inner layer needs to be comfortable against the skin. This layer may be made of cotton, silk, or synthetic materials such as polyester or microfiber.

- The middle layer, which could be more than one garment, needs to trap heat. Garments made of wool, fleece, down, polyester, or cotton keep warmth in.

- The outer layer could be a jacket or coat that keeps out the wind and rain. Warm shoes or boots keep feet protected, and a hat or scarf help to keep body heat in.

Wet-Weather Clothes

When it rains, people wear raincoats and use umbrellas to keep dry. Raincoats usually have holes or flaps to let the air circulate around the body, and to let out perspiration.

Cold-weather clothes keep body warmth in and cold out.

Women in India wear loose cotton saris to keep them cool.

Hot-Weather Clothes

In warm or hot weather, the most suitable clothes are made of lightweight materials such as cotton or linen, which have a fairly open weave. These materials absorb perspiration and allow air to flow around the body.

In hot weather, we need to protect ourselves from the Sun, as it can cause sunburn and heatstroke. This is very important in places with hot climates. Hats with wide brims and clothing with long sleeves protect us from sunburn.

White or light-colored clothes that reflect the Sun's **radiation** can keep us cooler than dark clothes. Sandals are more comfortable than shoes when it is hot.

Houses

Houses are often built to suit the climate. Different features are included to ensure the house is comfortable even in very cold or very hot weather.

Cold-Weather Houses

In cold weather, houses need to be well heated. Many have central heating, which sends warm air all through the house. People who live in very cold climates need to keep their houses warm all the time, or their water pipes can freeze. Houses in cold places often have thick walls and small windows.

Insulation

In cold weather, we need houses that keep the heat in. **Insulation** in the walls and ceilings keeps heat from escaping. Materials used for insulation include **fiberglass**, cotton, wool, synthetic **polymers**, cork, hemp, and straw. The most common kind of insulation in today's houses is fiberglass batts. Batts are large, flat, and soft blocks of material that are fitted into ceilings and walls.

In snowy places buildings usually have steep roofs so the snow can slide off when it gets too heavy.

Hot-Weather Houses

Houses in hot climates are often built to let air **circulate**. They may have open doors and windows. They may be built on stilts to let air circulate underneath, especially if the area also sometimes floods.

In some hot places, houses are built with thick walls to keep the heat out. They may be painted white to reflect the heat and to help keep them cool.

Wide verandas that surround a house provide shade from the Sun. Walls and roofs can be insulated. In hot weather, houses are kept cool by closing windows and doors and pulling down the curtains and blinds.

Weather Report

Sunlight can be used to make electricity, which is called solar power. Water can also be heated using heat from the Sun.

Stilt houses are built to let air circulate underneath and to survive floods.

Houses like these in Greece are common around the Mediterranean Sea where the summers are very hot.

9

Work

The weather affects the work many people do, sometimes helping and sometimes making jobs harder.

Farmers

Farmers all over the world provide our food. They rely on getting enough sunshine and water on their land to grow their crops and raise their animals. When there is bad weather such as **drought** or floods, their crops may fail and their animals may starve.

Farmers are experts on the weather. They know the right time of year to plant crops, so that the seeds will have enough light, warmth, and rain to **germinate** and grow. Farmers usually grow crops that are suited to the weather in their area. For example, rice grows in shallow water, so it is usually grown in places that receive a lot of rain. Crops can be grown in dry places by using **irrigation**.

Weather Report

Many farmers grow trees and shrubs to protect crops, animals, and the soil from wind. These groups of trees and shrubs are known as windbreaks.

Farmers prepare their land for sowing so they can plant crops when the weather conditions are suitable.

Aircraft Pilots

Aircraft pilots plan their flights, takeoffs, and landings around the weather. They cannot fly if there are severe thunderstorms, and they cannot land if there is thick fog.

Fishers

Fishers cannot go out in their boats if there is strong wind, because strong wind creates huge waves. Large waves can tip their boats over.

Ski-Lift Operators

Ski-lift operators work on the snowfields and help people ski. They rely on good snowfalls, or they cannot work.

Surf-lifeguards

Surf-lifeguards work at beaches and swimming pools and rescue swimmers in trouble. Surf-lifeguards often have to work in dangerous conditions, such as when it is windy or there are riptides in the sea.

This surf-lifeguard is watching swimmers at a surf beach.

11

Recreation

Bad weather conditions can often lead to fun for people. They rely on the weather for many kinds of sports and entertainment.

Snow Sports

Soft snow is the best kind for skiing and snowboarding. Soft snow is also good for playing on a bobsled or a toboggan. If the weather is very clear and sunny, the surface of the snow can melt during the day and then freeze overnight, which makes the snow hard, icy, and dangerous.

Ice-Skating and Racing

In some parts of Europe and North America, lakes freeze over in winter. Many people go ice-skating on these lakes. Sports such as ice hockey and speed skating grew in these areas. People even hold motorbike races on ice.

Ice skating on frozen lakes is a popular winter sport in the northern hemisphere.

Luge racers ride sleds down ice tracks at high speeds.

Sailing

People who sail yachts need winds that are strong enough to fill the sails but not so strong that the boats can be blown over. Sailing is also made dangerous by large waves. Sail boards and land sailers also need enough wind to fill their sails.

Gliding

Hang-gliders and plane-gliders need to find warm, rising **air currents** known as "thermals." These air currents form in places where the ground is warmed and the air is rising.

This hang-glider is being carried on a warm rising air current.

Weather Report

In car races such as Formula One, the teams have to put different tires on the cars for wet and dry weather, and the cars need to be driven more slowly in wet weather.

Land sailers need wind to fill their sails and blow them along.

13

Living with Thunderstorms

These bolts of lightning are jumping from the clouds to the ground.

During a thunderstorm people need to keep safe from the wind, **lightning**, **hail**, and even floods that can come with it.

Wind

Passengers and crew in aircraft can be injured if planes are thrown around by the strong **updrafts** and **downdrafts** that take place in thunderclouds. Sudden downdrafts can even slam planes into the ground while they are landing. This is why planes need to avoid severe thunderstorms.

People can also be hurt when the wind blows down walls or trees.

Lightning

Lightning is a huge electrical spark that flashes across the sky during thunderstorms. People need to find shelter when there is lightning about, because it is very dangerous. When lightning strikes the ground it can hit trees, buildings, people, and animals.

People are not safe anywhere outdoors when there is lightning, but beaches, water, and open fields are particularly dangerous. The best shelter is a building such as a house. If there is no way to get indoors, a car is the next best thing.

Hail

Hailstones are formed in a thunderstorm. They are balls of ice that grow as they are held up in the air by updrafts and downdrafts. Hail can injure people and damage cars and buildings. If hailstones are much larger than a pea it is important to find shelter.

Floods

Thunderstorms can cause sudden floods because there is often a lot of rain in a short time. This type of flood is known as a flash flood. Flash flooding is extremely dangerous. Floodwater from thunderstorms can sweep people away, especially children who are caught playing in a storm.

Weather Report

Hailstones larger than cricket balls have been observed.

Cumulonimbus clouds bring thunderstorms.

Living with Tornadoes

A tornado is a violent and extremely dangerous column of air that extends from a thunderstorm to the ground. Most tornadoes are about 246 feet (75 meters) wide and travel at speeds of up to 112 mi (180 km) per hour. They can destroy houses and large buildings, uproot trees, and throw cars hundreds of feet.

Tornadoes occur in many countries, but are most common in the midwestern part of the United States, in an area known as Tornado Alley.

Finding Shelter

People who live in tornado areas usually have a safety plan. This means that they go to a **basement** when there has been a tornado warning. If they can't find a basement, a ground-floor room such as a bathroom is the next safest place. People who live in tornado areas often have homes with basements and strong roofs and walls.

Tornadoes usually have a funnel shape.

Powerful tornadoes can suck up almost anything in their path.

Tornado Watch

Meteorologists use weather **radar** to give them information on developing storms. Weather officials mainly use radio and television to tell people there is danger from a tornado.

Tornado Spotters

There are volunteers who live in tornado areas who are trained as tornado spotters. If they observe a thundercloud that looks likely to produce a tornado, they report it to weather officials.

Tornado Alerts

People who live in tornado areas have systems to warn them of tornadoes. In North America, there are two main levels of alert about tornadoes.

- A tornado watch is given out if there is weather likely to lead to dangerous thunderstorms. People are asked to be on the lookout for coming storms.

- A tornado warning is given if a tornado has been seen or if there are thunderclouds that might form one. This is the time when people should move to their chosen safe place.

People are also warned about a coming tornado by tornado **sirens**, which are located in public places.

Parkersburg, Iowa, experienced tornado destruction in May 2008.

Tropical Storms

Tropical storms are called hurricanes, cyclones, and typhoons. Some people who live in areas that have tropical storms are able to move to shelters when a storm is coming. Many others cannot reach shelter, and may be killed or injured by the winds and floods that come with tropical storms.

Tropical storms bring violent thunderstorms, huge coastal waves, and floods. Wind speeds can reach 195 mi (314 km) per hour, or more. These winds uproot trees, and destroy houses and buildings. Tropical storms can cause billions of dollars worth of damage.

When a tropical storm is approaching, local emergency services and owners of buildings start preparing by boarding up windows and tying down outdoor equipment. People start moving to large buildings or specially built storm shelters. Sometimes, when officials believe the storm is going to be very severe, they **evacuate** the area.

Weather Report

Many thousands of people live on low-lying land in tropical areas, and are badly affected by large waves caused by tropical storms.

People can prepare for tropical storms if they have enough warning.

Storm Watch

Tropical storms always form over the sea, and meteorologists in storm-warning centers around the world look out for them. If they find one, they monitor it closely. Some tropical storms stay over the sea and others move toward land.

Storm Warnings

People who live on the coast and are in the path of a tropical storm are sent warnings as the storm gets closer. The warnings are sent mainly by radio and television broadcasts, and also by the Internet, telephone, and text message. Some coastlines have warning sirens along them, which warn people when the storm is about to reach them.

Weather Report

Weather officials have categories for tropical storms. Category five is the strongest, most violent storm. Category one storms only cause some damage to crops and trees.

This office building on the Mississippi coast was destroyed by Hurricane Katrina, a category three storm, in August 2005.

This satellite image shows Hurricane Andrew moving from east to west (right to left) on August 23, 24, and 25, 1992.

Extreme Climates

The Bedouin and Inuit are two groups of people who live in places with extreme climates. Extreme climates are extremely hot, cold, wet, dry, or windy.

The Bedouin

The Bedouin people live in the hot and dry deserts of North Africa and the Middle East. They move about the desert searching for food and water. They set up tents as they travel, which have one open side and are cool in the day. At night, the Bedouin light a fire inside their tents to keep them warm.

The Bedouin wear clothes that cover most of their bodies to protect them from the Sun, wind, and **sandstorms**. Their clothing is loose-fitting to help keep them cool. The desert is cold at night, so their clothes must also keep them warm.

Weather Report

The deserts where the Bedouin people live are the hottest in the world.

A Bedouin tent in the Sahara Desert, Morocco.

Bedouin clothes are loose and cover the body. A headscarf keeps moisture in to stop dehydration.

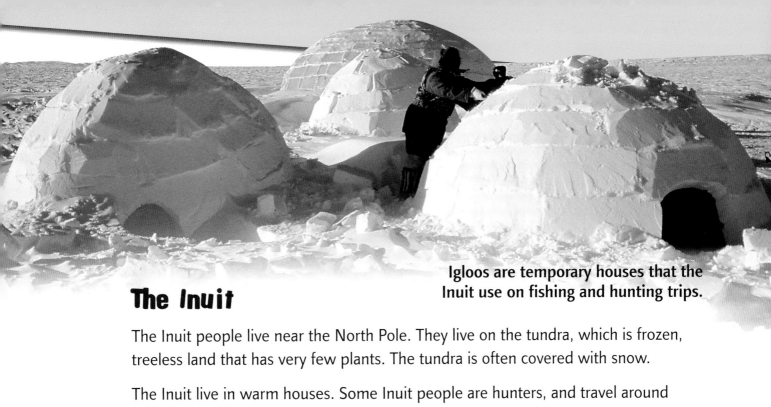

Igloos are temporary houses that the Inuit use on fishing and hunting trips.

The Inuit

The Inuit people live near the North Pole. They live on the tundra, which is frozen, treeless land that has very few plants. The tundra is often covered with snow.

The Inuit live in warm houses. Some Inuit people are hunters, and travel around hunting seals, polar bears, caribou (reindeer), and other animals. Sometimes hunters have to build igloos from blocks of snow. They stay in these for a few days at a time while they are away from their homes.

When Inuit people are outdoors in the cold for a long time, they wear clothing made from animal skins with fur. The outer garment is a parka with a hood.

Weather Report

The Inuit drive snowmobiles to get around. Children often ride to school in snowmobiles.

These Inuit children in Barrow, Alaska, are wearing traditional ceremonial parkas made of fur.

21

Animals and Weather

All animals have adapted to survive the weather conditions that they live in. This means that they have features or behaviors that help them live in their **environment**.

Animals in Hot Climates

Animals that live in hot deserts often live underground in burrows. They have strong front legs and claws that are good for digging. Some of them sleep through the summer. Others, such as desert toads, lie underground until the summer rains come.

Some warm-weather animals are only active at dawn or dusk, when it is cooler. Others, such as bats, rodents, foxes, and skunks, are nocturnal, which means they are only active during the night.

Ways that Animals Cope with Heat

Animals	Features that help them survive the heat
reptiles	tough **scales** to protect them from the hot ground
lizards	move extremely fast across hot surfaces, so they don't burn
camels	can survive for two weeks without water and a long time without food

This desert spiny lizard lives in the desert in the United States.

This marsupial mole burrows in Australian deserts. It is blind and has legs and feet made for digging. Look at its strong claws.

Animals in Cold Climates

Animals that live in cold places have thick fur to keep them warm. Their fur has a soft underlayer that provides insulation. Musk oxen have thick overcoats of shaggy, long, straight hair that hangs down to the ground. Their undercoats are thick brown fleece. Some of the coat is shed in the summer.

Ways that Animals Cope with the Cold

Animals	Features that help them survive the cold
bears and squirrels	sleep through the winter
walruses, whales, and seals	thick layer of fat called blubber to keep them warm
arctic hares	thick fur that changes color in the winter and in the summer

In the winter, musk oxen huddle together in groups for protection and to keep warm.

Weather Report

Animals and birds cope with rain because they have a waterproof coating on their fur or feathers.

King penguins have a thick layer of blubber as well as feathers to help them survive the freezing conditions.

Plants and Weather

Like animals, plants have adapted to survive the weather conditions that they live in.

Weather Report

The Arctic is very cold. Many plants that live there cope with the cold by being dark in color, being covered in hair, and growing in clumps.

Plants in Cold Climates

Conifers are trees with needlelike leaves that grow in snowy areas. The snow slides off the needles, which lets the trees get as much light as possible. The dark color of the needles allows them to absorb as much heat from the Sun as possible.

Trees in **deciduous** forests have thick bark to protect them against the cold winters.

Plants in Hot Climates

Plants such as bromeliads grow in hot **rain forest** areas. Their leaves are shaped to catch water. Insects and other small creatures get trapped in the water and provide **nutrition** for the plant. Many rain forest plants get more water than they need and have broad leaves so water can run off.

Cactuses are also suited to hot climates. They store water in their fleshy leaves.

Bromeliads are shaped to catch water.

These plants grow on the tundra near the North Pole.

Plants in Dry or Windy Climates

Plants in dry areas often have leaves that are tough, small, and waxy to keep water in. Hairs on leaves help to shade plants, and keep their water loss down. Some plants have leaves that turn throughout the day, so only the edges of the leaves face the Sun. This means there is less heat on the leaves.

Grass has narrow leaves to minimize water loss, and its soft stems allow different types of grass to bend easily in the wind. Grass often spreads its pollen by wind, so it is suited to growing in windy places. Grass that grows in dry places has long roots that reach deep down. This helps grass survive the tough periods.

Some plants, called succulents, store water in their stems or leaves.

Harnessing Weather

Many people now use the Sun and wind to make electricity. This kind of energy is also known as renewable energy, which means that the source of energy will not run out.

Solar Power

Solar power is electricity made from sunlight. People who live in areas with a lot of sunshine can use the Sun's light and heat to provide energy. Solar cells are laid out where they will catch sunlight and absorb the Sun's energy. Electricity flows out of wires that are connected to the solar cells.

The Sun's heat is collected and used to heat water as it travels through pipes, ready for household use.

Solar Hot Water

Many people heat their household water with solar heat. Water is heated by sending it through pipes laid out in a flat box where they will catch the Sun's heat. This hot water is then piped through a heating tank, where it heats up the household water.

Solar panels are made up of many solar cells.

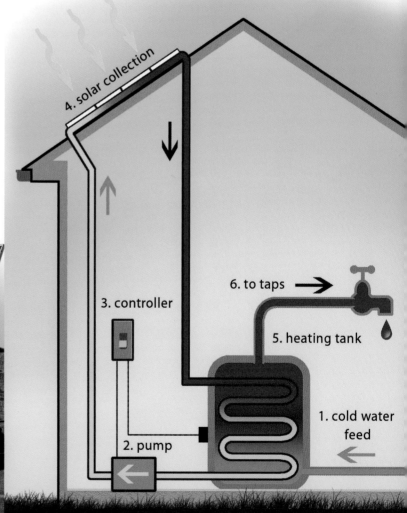

4. solar collection

6. to taps →

3. controller

5. heating tank

1. cold water feed

2. pump

Wind farms are often built on hills where there is plenty of wind.

Wind Power

Many communities in very windy areas are building wind farms to make electricity. The wind turns the arms of electricity **generators**. This electricity becomes part of the area's electricity supply.

Wave Power

Electricity can also be made from the power of waves in the ocean. Buoys that float on the ocean ride up and down on the waves. The moving buoys cause electricity generators to spin. The electricity that is made is called wave power.

Weather Talk

Throughout time, people have talked about the weather. They have told stories about weather gods and they have sayings to explain weather.

Weather Stories

In ancient India, people said that a dragon guarded the clouds to stop the rain from falling. They cheered for the storm god to coax the dragon away from the cloud, so that rain could fall.

Many ancient Africans believed that people who were hit by lightning were being punished by angry gods.

According to one tribe of American Indians, the sky god wore clothes made of clouds. When he spread his arms, his clothes stretched across the whole sky.

An Indigenous Australian story says that frost comes from the stars of the Seven Sisters. The sisters once lived on Earth but they were so cold that they sparkled with icicles. They flew up into the sky and once each year they pull off their icicles and throw them down to Earth.

Thor was the Norse god of thunder. He had a hammer that he threw to make the sound of thunder. The day called Thursday was named after him.

Weather Sayings

People have many sayings about the weather. There is one for nearly every type of weather condition.

No weather's ill if the wind be still.

Cold is the night when the stars shine bright.

Red sky at night, sailor's delight.
Red sky in morning, sailor take warning.

Clear moon, frost soon.

A rainbow afternoon
Good weather coming soon.

Rain before seven, fine before eleven.

When clouds appear like rocks and towers, the Earth will be washed by frequent showers.

When clouds look like black smoke, a wise man will put on his cloak.

Moss dry, sunny sky; moss wet, rain we'll get.

When dew is on the grass, rain will never come to pass.

Weather Wonders

The Sahara is the largest hot desert in the world, and it has a population of 2.5 million people.

Tornadoes occur on every continent except Antarctica.

Hurricane Katrina, which struck New Orleans in August 2005, was the most costly tropical storm in the world. It caused $81.2 million of property damage, and the amount for all damages combined totaled $100 billion. It killed 1,836 people.

Female polar bears dig dens in the snow where they **hibernate** during the worst part of the winter. Their cubs are born in the den.

Solar-powered cars can travel at 56 mi (90 km) per hour or more.

Glossary

air currents gentle movements of air

basement a room that is below ground level

circulate move around freely

deciduous trees that lose their leaves in the fall

downdrafts strong downward winds

drought a period of less rain than normal, usually lasting months or years

environment our surroundings; the earth, air, and living things around us

evacuate move people out of an area, usually because there is danger

fiberglass fibers made of glass

forecast predict something

generators machines that make electricity

germinate begin to grow from a seed

hail balls of ice that fall from thunderclouds

hibernate sleep through winter

insulation material that does not allow heat to pass through in the summer and retains warmth in the winter

irrigation watering crops and land using pumps, pipes, sprinklers, or channels

lightning a bright flash of electricity produced during a thunderstorm

meteorologists scientists who study weather

nutrition food

polymers fibers made of plastic

radar equipment that sends out signals to detect how far away something is

radiation energy, such as light and heat, that comes from the Sun

rain forest forest that gets a lot of rain

sandstorms windstorms that carry a large amount of sand

scales small, hard plates on the skin of reptiles

sirens loudspeakers that make a very loud wailing sound

solar cells devices that absorb the Sun's energy to make electricity

synthetic made by humans

thunderstorm storm that brings thunder and lightning.

tropical the area of land on and around Earth's equator

updrafts strong upward winds

Index